Divine Interventions ... Messages Of Hope

E.M. Schick

www.trafford.com

North America & international
toll-free: 1 888 232 4444 (USA & Canada)
phone: 250 383 6864 ♦ fax: 812 355 4082

ACKNOWLEDGEMENTS

Big thanks to Donna Williams who diligently sacrificed hours of her time to proof read my work. She was my first friend and is to this day, a blessing. I also want to thank Judy Lindberg for her grammatical nudging. Her opinion based on years of experience was greatly appreciated.

Lord…all that we have accomplished you have done for us. (Isaiah 26:12) NKJV

INTRODUCTION:

Divine Interventions...Messages of Hope, is an account of the times that God has shown me just how personally He wants to be involved in my life. I believe that He speaks intimately to each of us, but if we do not pause long enough and listen, we may miss His message. It is my wish that you find hope from these true stories and be reminded that we are not alone in this earthly journey.

Our Father and our future are from above; therefore we need to have hope.

"Do not remember the former things,
Nor consider the things of old.
Behold, I will do a new thing,
Now it shall spring forth;
Shall you not know it?
I will even make a road in the wilderness
And rivers in the desert"
(Isaiah 43:8) NKJV

CONTENTS

THE BABY THAT FLEW AWAY

It was 12:30 pm, June 6ᵗʰ, 1980. I had put my younger son, Christian, who had just celebrated his first birthday, in his crib for a nap. My four year old son, Nathan (NJ), and I walked around the inside of the house to close the windows. The sky outside had become very dark and the wind had picked up. I glanced out the window of our fourteen month old ranch style home and saw the newly planted red maple sapling bent over and nearly lying on the ground. I really didn't give it much thought at the time. NJ and I headed to the master bedroom in the rear of the house. He stood within the door frame as I walked over to close the window. When I was about three feet away from the wall, the ceiling started to collapse down onto the top of my head. As I lifted my arms up to protect myself, the bottom of the window flew out of the wall and slammed into the left side of my forehead. Although this blow to my head knocked me unconscious, I still recall tumbling in mid air in the fetal position. My flight only lasted a few seconds and ended with me slamming my right shoulder and hip into the ground. There was a light drizzle of rain falling and the sprinkles of water started to bring me back to consciousness. When I heard NJ calling "Mommy, Mommy," I staggered to my feet. I was dazed, my forehead was stinging, and my vision was blurred. I later realized that I had lost my glasses. I followed NJ's voice to locate him. He was six feet away, standing in a pile of rubble up to his shoulders. His arms were pinned at his side; he couldn't move. As I tried to reach him, I had to climb through layers of broken drywall and remnants of the floors. The bedroom rugs were still stapled to the ripped sheets of plywood. I had heard stories of how in times of danger one's capability of moving heavy objects could increase. On that day, without a second thought, I picked up and tossed aside fragments of our home that I know I would not have been able to move at any other time. Within two feet of reaching NJ, I stretched one arm over and grabbed him by the front of his tee shirt. I lifted him straight up into the air, and he did not have a scratch on him! My next thought was to find Christian. As I turned around, I found myself looking down into the basement. There, my St. Bernard, named Gertie, stood next to a broken water line which sprayed a ten foot arc into the air. The entire house had been ripped off the foundation and thrown twenty feet onto the hill side that was once my backyard.

Stunned, I looked at NJ and said, "We are going to sue those builders for our new house falling down." I remember thinking that a fourteen month old house should be able to withstand some wind! I took him by the hand and paced back and forth looking at the large pile of rubble. I could not comprehend that I was looking at the remains of my house. In my state of shock, I went from laughing and thinking that this is not real, and I will soon wake up, to telling my four year old son that his baby brother had to be dead! For several minutes we aimlessly walked around the foundation looking for Chris. Broken glass cut my bare feet. My now throbbing head pain and the inability to see clear, made me realize that I needed help. We walked across the street to our neighbors. I knocked on the front door, and when Angie answered, she just stared at me. I was covered with a layer of blown-in insulation and my face was bloody. She had no idea who I was. I said "Please take Nathan inside, my house blew away, and I can't find my baby." Angie looked across the street and saw that my house was gone. She started to scream to her husband Bob for help. Bob and his teenage son, Tony ran across the street to help find Chris.

Within a few minutes, strangers were stopping their cars and jumping out to help. I heard people yelling, "A baby flew away" as they ran several yards behind the rubble into the wooded area. The high voltage lines that ran next to the house had sheets of insulation dangling from them like tangled kites. Bob asked when the storm had hit, where Chris was in the house? I said that he was in his crib, for a nap. He asked what the color of Chris' bedroom rug was, hoping that he could find remnants and start his search from there. I had no idea of the rug color. A crowd of ten to fifteen people were running around screaming at each other in panic. I was standing next to the fifteen foot high pile of debris, and I heard a soft, single "hmm" sound. I have no doubt that Chris's guardian angel was getting my attention. I called to Bob, and he and Tony ran to my side. I said, "He's under there," as I pointed to a tee-pee looking pile of floors, windows and walls. Bob looked at me in disbelief. I'm sure now that he thought that I must be out of my mind to think that anyone could survive being buried under all this weight, let alone a baby. Bob called to others for help, and three men stooped under the "I" beam and hoisted it upward with their backs. Young Tony dug through the rubble in the area which I had pointed to. Just then, Tony's foot broke through a glass window that he was standing on, lacerating his ankle. He ignored the pain because as he looked down through the glass, something caught his eye. The next thing I heard was Tony saying, "I see a leg." I wanted to know if it was connected to a body. As he reached down into the rubble, he said he was not sure. Chris' crib mattress was bent around him in a "U" shape protecting him on all sides. Across Chris' chest laid a large set of rosary beads that my mother had given to me years before when I was sick in the hospital. When Chris was born and we brought him home from the hospital, I hung the beads on his bedroom dresser, across the room from his crib. Those beads were given to me at a time when I was frightened and needed help. And on the day of the storm, when I had never been more frightened and in need of help, God gave me this sign that he was watching over me and my children. As Chris was lifted out, his body was limp and his eyes were rolled back. I could see that he was unconscious as he was handed to me. I reached into his mouth to clear his airway of powdery particles of insulation. His breathing was very shallow and his pulse was rapid. He had a laceration on his forehead that bled slowly. I remember saying that he must be bleeding internally, and that he was in shock. It was obvious to everyone that we needed to get to a hospital.

Back in 1980, cellular networks were just being developed and it wasn't until the mid 80's that we started to see "car phones", so helpful strangers ran in every direction from house to house to see if anyone had an active land line. The lines were down for several city blocks, but eventually they reached one that was operative. After dialing 911 and speaking to a police officer, a Good Samaritan came back to report that the officer had told him that they were receiving several calls. A trailer court had one hundred trailers destroyed and a department store's front windows were blown out, injuring numerous shoppers. The officer told him that several of the roads in our area were closed off due to debris and fallen trees. He instructed the caller to drive me and my sons to the closest hospital, and if the roads were blocked, he was to drive on residential lawns. The police car would be waiting five miles down the road to escort us to the hospital.

I don't recall getting into the car, but I know that I was sitting in the front seat, holding Chris in my arms, and Nathan sat between me and the driver. As I looked down at Chris, I became frantic. There was bright red blood all over his face. The driver, (and I still do not know his name) informed me that the blood was mine; my forehead laceration was dripping down onto Chris. Nothing else was said. The police officer met us as planned and within a few minutes we were arriving at the emergency room. As we walked through the door a nurse swooped down and grabbed Chris from me and took him into an exam room. When they took him for x-rays, they placed NJ and me into the nurse's lounge area. The rest of the exam rooms were filling up with victims from the trailer court and shopping center. A young frightened nurse's aide was placed in the lounge to "watch us," Even without my glasses, I could see her fear of anticipating what I might do. Her eyes' were wide open; she never seemed to blink. We could hear screaming and crying in the corridor, and every so often, a nurse would stick her head in the door and report "That's not your baby crying!" and in a flash she was gone again. I thought to myself, "I know my baby's cry, and that's not it!" In fact, I never heard Chris cry.

I was instructed to shower, and if my day wasn't going bad enough already, I was given enema soap to wash away insulation and blood. I dressed in hospital gowns, one open in the back, the other I wore as a robe. Chris was being x-rayed from head to toe. A nurse popped in to tell me that she wanted to contact my husband. I immediately informed her that it couldn't be done. I explained that he was an engineer for a Rail Road Company, and that he was somewhere on a train. There was a protocol for contacting employees which involved a lengthy phone tree. It was a difficult process and I certainly did not have any names or numbers to give her. I knew it was hopeless! It wasn't five minutes later that another employee stuck her head in the door and said, "Your husband work for the Rail Road? So does mine!" In a very short time I was talking to Dave on the phone. I told him that the house had been hit by a storm. Not wanting to upset him, I explained that a few of the windows in the house were blown out, and that there was a little damage. He said that he would be home as soon as possible, but it would probably take at least three hours.

A short visit from an ER doctor assured me that Chris was stable. He said that it was lucky that he was knocked unconscious. "If he would have cried and tried to take deep breaths, chances are he would have choked on the insulation and suffocated." Yes, God does works in strange ways. In this case it involved an unconscious baby who laid within a molded mattress for protection. In the meantime, my father- in- law arrived, and once the three of us were cleared to leave, he drove me and the boys back from the hospital. Luckily, my in-laws lived around the corner from me because I had no home to go to.

Dave made arrangements to take a cab home. At the end of the two and a half hour ride, as they drove up the hill on our street, the driver said, "Was that your house?...You don't owe me a cent!." I was standing on our lot, when Dave came up to me and said, "Where are my boys?" He ran up the hill to his parent's home to see our sons. He could not believe that they could have survived.

In the weeks that followed, I would walk around the rubble and try my best to understand what had happened. The "I" beam that supported my house was bent, but yet my children were alive. Hundreds of three inch nails protruded from wooden planks and my dishwasher was thrown fifty feet into my neighbor's garden. Twenty inch shards of glass were found embedded into the lawn, but yet my children were alive. How could this be? My mind could not make sense of it.

I recall that it was important when the insurance agent informed us that the storm was determined an act of God. This meant that our home owner's insurance would cover us. We were not covered for high wind damage. If the winds had not reached the speed that they did that day, we would have been without insurance coverage.

Clean-up was a massive task. Several neighbors offered support and help that was needed. Two envelopes filled with cash and good wishes were delivered by a kind woman who cried as she shared the concerns of those who had contributed. Some gathered our dirty clothing that they found on the ground and took them to the dry cleaners. One side of my neighbor's driveway was lined with a row of large pine trees. The top four feet of each tree was found in my basement. A high school teacher that lived up the street came every day, all day, for six weeks with a hammer in his hand. He was a quiet man who would ask what he was able to help with for the day. At dusk, he would disappear only to show up the next morning to do it all over again. For three weeks, a married couple who lived a mile down the road, came to offer their help. I remember when I first met Sam, he said, "You don't know me, and I don't know you, but anyone who had this happen to them, we want to help. Our truck is your truck." His wife would show up with a surgical mask on. One day my curiosity got the best of me and when I asked Sam why she wore a mask, he explained that she was allergic to the insulation, but still wanted to help. The Red Cross provided money to purchase a pair of shoes and an outfit for each of us. They also covered our basement with a large tarp to protect our washer and dryer.

Not everyone was good hearted, though. We had twenty-one sheets of plywood stored in our basement that we had purchased with plans of finishing off our game room. Two weeks after the tornado destroyed our home and everything with it, we were robbed. Someone came in the middle of the night and took all twenty-one sheets of plywood!

Try to imagine how I felt when I was asked by the insurance company to write down everything that I had in my house, down to the pictures on the walls, and estimate what it had cost us. I found myself looking through a catalog to stimulate my recall. There were items like the antique Christmas bulbs that were my grandmothers. How do you put a price on that? After weeks of this straining task, the insurance company took the list and depreciated everything on it. The check we received went directly back to the bank to pay for the house. We had the check in our hands just long enough to sign it.

A local newspaper reporter who wanted to write an article on the tornado asked, "How I was able to deal with the tragedy that had happened?" My response was that I did not consider what had happened to us a tragedy. It was a major inconvenience. Even though we had lost all our material possessions, I still had my children, and we were healthy. I did have a pleasant surprise when we found the night stand from our bedroom; the drawers were smashed in, locking them in place. When we broke it apart, I found several photos of my family and my wedding album with minimal water damage. I felt like I had found a treasure.

About four weeks after the storm, we attended a meeting for the tornado victims. One man had a broken leg and walked with crutches. Many of the survivors shared horrid stories of the individual devastation to their lives. But all agreed that we were grateful that no one had been killed. Several residents from the trailer camp reported that they did not have insurance and were living in hotel rooms. We were given information regarding loans that were offered to those who qualified by the United States Small Business Administration (SBA) to rebuild their homes.

Recovery from such an event can be a long and trying experience. I had taken Christian to the pediatrician for a follow-up visit. I told her that Chris had been crying excessively every day when I put him in bed for a nap. She told me that he probably remembered something about what happened and associated it with sleep. When I asked how long the crying would lasts, she said that it could be up to two years. It was two years to the day! I was so relieved when his crying bouts ended. This meant no more touching the walls and sadly saying, "Wall fall down?"

Lightening storms never use to bother me, but after the tornado it was a different story. When I heard thunder, the hair would stand up on the nap of my neck. I would start to sweat and shake. Two months after the storm, we visited the site of a friend's house that was in the early stage of construction. The builder had just blown the insulation into the walls. The smell of the insulation was a trigger to my memory and I was emotionally right back to the day of the storm. Similar anxiety attacks lasted three years.

You may be wondering about Nathan and how this affected him. Nathan said that he was totally awake when he flew through the air. He ended up with a small scratch on his arm. He was actually upset that he didn't have more dramatic evidence of what he had been through. In day care, the staff would play tornado, and he was able to tell his story. His only concern was for the brand new swing set that was now just twisted scrap metal. We reassured him that it would be replaced. Then he made one request, and that was to have a green rug in his new room. We assured him that it would not be a problem.

Twenty-eight years later, on the night before Christian's wedding, we gathered for the rehearsal dinner. In the invitations that I had sent out to the guests, I asked them to share any stories they may have about Linzy and Chris. I told a short story about the baby that flew away, and how his guardian angel had led us in his rescue. I shared that I had thought that God had saved Christian for me, to spare a mother the pain of the loss of a child.

9

But on that night, it was clear that I was wrong. As I saw the love in my son's eyes for his future wife I realized that God had saved Chris for Linzy. We raised our glasses, and with teary eyes; I gave thanks to God for all the angels that have blessed our lives.

Psalm 121, NKJV
I will lift up my eyes to the hills-
From whence comes my help?
My help comes from the Lord,
Who made heaven and earth.

He will not allow your foot to be moved;
He who keeps you will not slumber.
Behold, He who keeps Israel
Shall neither slumber nor sleep.

The Lord is your keeper;
The Lord is your shade at your right hand.
The sun shall not strike you by day,
Nor the moon by night.

The Lord shall preserve you from all evil;
He shall preserve your soul.
The Lord shall preserve your going out and your coming in.
From this time forth, and even forevermore.

GARAGE ANGELS

Less than four weeks after our home was destroyed by a tornado, we moved into a rental house. With no furniture we threw a slip cover over an old couch donated by a friend of the family and placed our mattresses on the floor. I was still somewhat in shock, but nevertheless, it was time to meet with home builders and attempt to get our lives back on track.

One evening, after viewing a model home, my husband and I discussed the pros and cons of what the builder had to offer. It was around 10:00 pm that we started our thirty mile drive home. We found ourselves on a winding country road and our car just stopped dead. No power, no lights, nothing. It now became obvious to us just how dark it was. The moon was not visible and we could not see our hands in front of our faces. It was pitch black!

There were no houses or lights in sight, and we were discussing whether we would walk together on the side of the road or my husband would leave me in the car to wait. We did not know how many miles that we would need to walk. I became frightened and was telling him that I did not want him to leave me, just then the inside of the car became filled with light. We turned around to find two large blinding headlights directly behind us. The vehicle seemed to come out of nowhere. My husband opened his door and got out of the car. I could see several silhouettes in the dark surrounding him. They exchanged a few words and then pulled their vehicle in front of ours. In moments they had our car hooked up to their truck and hoisted on its rear wheels. This is when I noticed that it was a tow truck! What were the odds that a tow truck would come upon us on a deserted country road at 10:00 at night?

My husband told me to get out of the car and get into the front seat of the truck. I could now see that all four of these guys were dressed in dirty blue jeans, torn denim vests and jackets. Their hair was long and greasy and they reeked of oil. Without speaking a word, three of them jumped on the rear of the truck. I thought to myself that this must be some kind of a set up. I kept wondering where they had come from.

I slid into the middle between the driver and my husband and we were off! Speeding down the dark road, I saw no lights, no homes or businesses. As we rode we made small talk. The stranger said he had a garage that was not too far away. The next thing I knew he was making a sharp right turn onto another old winding road. There were no road signs, no buildings or street lights, just open fields.

The farther we went, the more frightened I became. I had my right hand on my husband's left knee and I started to squeeze tightly out of fear. I did not know what was going through my husband's mind, but I was very nervous. I prayed a quick prayer for God's help to keep us safe. We drove for at least ten minutes, and did not see one other car on the road. We came up to fields on both sides of the road that were filled with skeletons of disassembled cars. This auto graveyard just increased my fear. My imagination went wild. I thought, if they wanted to kill us, they could easily hide our vehicle in this car graveyard, dispose of our bodies and no one would know the difference. We had left no trail. No one knew where we were or what had happened to us. It was the perfect setup if we were going to be taken advantage of.

As we drove a little farther, he pointed to an old Victorian house that was sitting up on the hill on the left side of the road. It resembled the house featured in the movie "Psycho." "That's where I live. I was supposed to get married but my fiancée cancelled the wedding." Oh Great, I thought, I bet this guy hates all women. I'm really in trouble. Over on the right side of the road was a one story cinder block building with two garage doors that were open. As we pulled up to the building and stopped, four more similar looking guys came out of the garage. Together they took our car off the tow hook and pushed it into the first garage bay. They didn't say too much but swarmed like a pit crew under the car's hood.

After a few minutes, one of them offered me a seat on a wobbly old wooden chair, while another opened an old dented refrigerator and offered me a can of Coke and my husband a beer. The driver told the others that we had lost our house in the tornado. One of them asked if we knew the people who had lost their baby in the storm. When we said that was us, they could not believe it. They had heard on the TV and read the stories in the newspaper, and they wanted to know all the details of what had happened. They asked how our sons were doing, and wondered what we were doing out there this late at night.

Two or three stayed focused on our car and they quickly identified the problem. The owner said that he would be able to fix it but needed to get to one of the cars in the junk yard for spare parts. He would need to wait for daylight. We used the garage's business phone to call our brother-in-law who came half way out and met us at a local convenience store. The owner of the garage offered to drive us to the rendezvous and told us that he would phone us the next day.

The next afternoon we received the call. My husband made arrangements for a ride out to the garage. When he arrived the car was ready, and the owner informed him that there was no charge. Instead, he gave his business card and said, "All I ask is that if you know someone who needs a mechanic, give them my name."

I must admit that I was embarrassed by my stereotyping. I had never considered myself a prejudiced person, but I had judged these guys based on how they dressed.

When I look back, I realize that they arrived out of nowhere, quietly did exactly what we needed them to do and asked nothing in return. These guys did not attract attention to themselves; they silently went about their business. They had a mission to accomplish and that is exactly what they did. The Garage Angels were polite, kind and thoughtful. I see how we were stranded and I was frightened, but the Lord came through for us. I had started to pray to God. I just asked for help, nothing specific. Sometimes just a simple, help me, is all that is needed. Thank you God for dirty, smelly Garage Angels!

> "God created humankind in his image…
> And indeed, it was very good."
> (Genesis 1:27-31) NKJV

BIG BERTHA

Following a yearly mammogram I received a call from my gynecologist telling me that my results showed a suspicious precancerous growth in my left breast. I scheduled to meet with a surgeon who decided that I would need to have a wedge section removed. When I reported for the surgery, I was first taken to the x-ray department. There I was told that a wire would have to be inserted into my breast. This "J" wire, named because of the end curvature which was placed around the growth, enabled the surgeon to locate the microscopic tissue that needed to be removed.

I was told that the wire would be inserted while my breast was compressed in the mammogram machine, for proper location. I was also told that I would not be able to have a local anesthesia, because this would blur the film.

It took over an hour with me standing while my breast was compressed in the machine. It was extremely painful and at times I thought that I might faint. To make matters worse, if I did faint, I knew that I would be unable to fall to the floor.

Because my breast had to remain compressed in the x-ray device, a young aide would come into the room and sit with me while the films were being read. Several films shot from different angles and increased magnification were taken. After thirty more minutes of prep, it was time for the wire insertion. While I stood, leaning forward, with my left breast horizontally compressed on the plastic clamp, the Radiologist inserted the wire into the lower side of my breast. Another film shot was taken to establish wire placement, and after several painful repositioning attempts, the exterior portion of the wire was cut off. Left behind was approximately two inches of wire, which was then covered with a small paper cup secured with two strips of surgical tape. This temporarily prevented the wire from becoming dislodged as I was taken to surgery. All went well with the surgical procedure and I was released from the hospital without complications.

For three weeks after the surgery, my left breast was swollen and bluish in color, a normal post-operative response. Due to the difference in size from my right breast, I dubbed my left "Big Bertha". When friends and family would call to check on my recovery, they would ask how Big Bertha was doing. My six week follow-up mammogram was clear and I was instructed to have mammograms every six months.

Six months later, my mammogram revealed that I once again had suspicious growths that needed to be removed, in the same breast.

This time when I reported for surgery, I knew what to expect. I was very nervous. While in the mammogram room I was told several times by the doctor that they needed to take extra shots and magnify them. This had happened quite frequently during my routine mammograms but I became very apprehensive just thinking of the pain that was to come from the wire insertion. I was told to have a seat on a metal stool in the room while the Radiologist examined the film. As I sat alone, my right leg started to shake up and down uncontrollably. I felt very frightened, and I glanced over to the right side of the room. There was another metal stool pushed against the wall. I pictured my guardian angel, Lily, sitting on the stool watching over me, and I spoke out loud to her. "Lily, just make it a little less painful than last time," I begged, with tears in my eyes. I continued to pray silently and after ten minutes the Radiologist came into the room and asked me to follow her because she wanted to show me something. As we walked into the viewing room, I saw two walls full of film prints of Big Bertha. With over thirty views, the doctor started to explain. "Here are shots of your breast six months ago prior to your surgery, and here are the films six weeks after your surgery." While comparing them, she pointed out that she could see that the mass was successfully removed. She then moved to the films that were just taken a few weeks ago, and located a mass that she described as a suspicious abnormal growth. Lastly she reviewed the films taken that day. She moved her finger from film to film, pointing to 10 different views, and said. "This type of growth does not get reabsorbed, it just doesn't go away! I can't explain what has happened, there is nothing there!" I looked at her with a smile on my face and said, "I can." Her face had a questionable expression. "The Lord has healed me!" I said. She immediately responded, "It has to be a miracle, I have no other explanation, and I can't find any reason to recommend that you should have this surgical procedure today."

I walked back into my hospital room where my husband was waiting. Surprised to see me back so soon, he questioned me as to what had happened. All I could tell him was that the Lord had healed me and we were going home.

I could not stop smiling. I know that my guardian angel is always with me, but once again she communicated to me just how loving and intimate God wants to be with us. I was blessed to see how God wants to touch us each at a very personal level.

God placed a guardian at our side. She is capable of helping us in ways that we cannot imagine; she is just waiting for you to call upon her.

> I sought the Lord, and He heard me, and delivered me from all my fears.
> They looked to Him and were radiant, and their faces were not ashamed.
> This poor man cried out, and the Lord heard him, and saved him out of all his troubles.
> The angel of the Lord encamps all around those who fear him, and delivers them.
> Oh, taste and see that the Lord is good; blessed is the man who trusts in Him!
> (Psalm 34: 4-8)NKJV

CALLED BY NAME

I had been putting off going to visit my father and step mother for almost a month. Five weeks had passed since my husband of twenty-eight years had unexpectedly walked out on me. I had fallen into a deep depressive state and I knew that I would have to face my father at some point. I was calling him every other day, but I usually would visit him weekly. Dad was very close to my husband; he loved him as a son. I had decided that it was not yet the right time to tell Dad that he had left me. I knew that my step mother was being treated for depression, and I did not feel that I could handle the emotional strain of trying to explain something that I had no answers for myself. I pulled myself together emotionally and decided that a visit was inevitable. Within five minutes of arriving, dad asked me what was wrong. As I tried to explain, he questioned me as to what I had done and whether he had left me for another woman. I had no answers. I left feeling extremely sad and I cried all the way home.

I decided to stop at my parish church; this is where I often found comfort. I sat in the front row of the dark church praying for God to speak to me. As I sat there I remembered something that had happened to me twenty years earlier. My mother was on an oncology ward for the last week of her life. I was an ICU nurse, at the hospital, and I would come and spend time with my mom on my dinner break and after work. One day as I walked down the hall to her room, a woman came up to me and said, "I have to tell you what just happened to my husband." I was not sure if she wanted to talk to me because I was wearing hospital scrubs, or because she had seen me visiting my mother's room. She then explained that her husband was also a patient on that unit and that his room was across the hall from my mom's.

Earlier that day when she arrived to visit him he was not in his room. So she walked down to the end of the hall to a small chapel. She looked in and saw her husband sitting in the front pew talking with another man. She did not want to interrupt and decided to go back to his room to wait for him. He soon returned and she asked who the man was that he was talking with. He said, "He was an angel! I was praying and told God that I was frightened to die. Just then, the angel walked up to me and told me not to worry. God had sent him to tell me that I would not be alone, that he would be with me all the time." She described that her husband was smiling and commented that she had not seen him smile in a very long time. He was no longer afraid to die.

While I was sitting in church I remembered this story and I pleaded to God. I told Him that I did not expect Him to send an angel to walk in and sit down next to me. But I needed a sign that would assure me that He heard me and would help me through the pain. At the end of my prayers, I headed home.

When I arrived home, my heart was aching. I sat on my living room sofa and sobbed. I felt abandoned, my feelings were crushed, and I really did not know how I was going to survive the pain. When I was unable to produce any more tears, I sat and stared for several minutes. It was at that time that I remembered that a Healing Mass was going to be held at a nearby church. I could not remember the specifics but I found the church bulletin which confirmed that it was that same evening; in fact, it was starting in one hour. I had been to the church once before so I thought I could find it without any difficulty.

I jumped into my car and when I arrived at the church I noticed a large crowd of people walking from the parking lot into the rear entrance. As I walked in, I could see approximately two hundred people, who were headed to the front of the church. I looked around, but I did not recognize anyone. I sat in the back pew by myself. I had never been to a Healing Mass and did not know what to expect. In the front of the church was a gentleman playing the guitar while two women sang. We were given booklets of song lyrics so we could sing along. I was still very upset and found that I was unable to focus enough to read the words. I felt tormented. I wanted to sing, so I prayed to God to help me get everything out of the Mass that He wanted me to. I began to sing and give God praise which filled me with peacefulness. After several uplifting songs, a procession of priests and altar boys walked down the center isle. I did not recognize any of the ten priests who then sat on the altar facing the parishioners. Once the Mass was started, I decided that I wanted to do whatever I could to receive the full benefit of the service. Until then I did not feel comfortable drinking the wine from the cup, but during communion I took the wine for the first time. All old habits were questionable at this time, so I was opened for change.

On completion of the Mass, one priest introduced himself as a Healing Priest. He explained that he traveled from church to church, holding Healing Masses. He went on to say that for those of us who have been to a Healing Mass, we would know how it was going to go. I thought to myself that leaves me out, as this was all new to me.

Then he picked up a notebook that looked like a shorthand pad and said that while he was praying, the Lord instructed him to do some specific healing. He explained that if he said something that applied to us, we could raise our hand and claim the blessing. Others who were around us could place their hands on us and give praise to God for the blessings that we were receiving. He went on to say that he would understand if we did not want to put our hands up, because some of the things that he would say may cause some embarrassment. He reassured us that just because he might not identify our specific need, it did not mean that God was not healing. He reminded us that God was bigger than that, and that He knows all our needs. As he read from his notes he said that there was someone whose left eye was cloudy and needed vision surgery. He added that God would heal this person. As he said this, an elderly gentleman put up his hand and those around him laid hands on his shoulders and praised the Lord.

The priest continued his list of ailments such as the inability to walk for more than four steps because a right knee is frozen, the inability to walk because they had breathing problems, someone suffered with left leg pain and another had ear problems. People continued to lift their hands and give God praise. He mentioned that someone's grandson had been caught with drugs, and God was healing him.

He had gone through about a dozen ailments when he said that someone is having marriage problems, and I raised my hand along with ten other people. I said to myself, this is why I'm here! I thanked God for the blessing that I now felt had been given to me.

The priest continued with his list and he had gone through roughly thirty different conditions when he said, "There is an Elaine." WHAT! I said to myself. I could not believe my ears. In a split second several thoughts ran through my mind. I was convinced that my mind was playing tricks on me. There was no way that he said my name. "There is an Elaine...Elaine?" He repeated. I tried to raise my arm, but I found myself weak and unable to lift my trembling hand. Tears started to run down my face. I looked around at the remainder of the attendees and no one else had raised their hand. Out of two hundred plus people, I was the only Elaine. He looked to the back of the church and said, "Elaine, God is healing what you asked for" I still did not believe this. In the pew in front of me sat a young woman with her two children. She turned to me and said "Are you Elaine?" When I nodded my head yes, she said "Praise the Lord!" He called me by name, and this woman also heard it, so I wasn't imagining it. I had asked God for a sign, and sure enough, he answered my request.

When I left the church, I was elated, and yet a bit doubtful. I immediately called an old roommate who belonged to the same church years ago. I asked if she had put my name on a prayer list, but she had not. I asked if she knew any of the priests that were there. She assured me that she had not been to that church in over five years.

I was now convinced that my husband would soon return to me. But I was wrong. I had a tough lesson to learn. I had to realize that God's ways are greater than my ways. He sees the whole picture, while I have minute glimpses. It took me several years to accept the fact that just because my marriage did not turn out like I had planned, it did not mean God was not healing. I believe that the years I spent wishing and hoping for my old life to return, were the devil's way of holding me back from moving forward with my life. I was told that God would heal my marriage. I assumed that meant that my husband would return and we would fix all our problems. That was my interpretation, not God's. He brought me through it in a way that only He was able to. He knew what was in my best interest and what I truly needed.

I have heard people say that we should not ask God for signs, and that doing so is a sign of a lack of faith. All I know is that at a time when I needed to hear from my Godly Father, He let me know in a very matter of fact way. He called me by name.

> "... Fear not, for I have redeemed you;
> I have called you by your name;
> You are Mine.
> When you pass through the waters, I will be with you;
> And through the rivers, they shall not overflow you.
> When you walk through the fire, you shall not be burned.
> Nor shall the flame scorch you."
> (Isaiah 43:1-2) NKJV

> "The Sheep hear His voice.
> He calls His own sheep by name and leads them out"
> (John 10:33) NKJV

ALL SIDES

Less than three months after my marital separation my father died suddenly. Even though Dad was 86 years old, he was a healthy and independent individual. I would talk with him and his wife weekly and found comfort in knowing that he was enjoying his latter years. A few months later, my St Bernard became ill and I had to have her put down. Sydney was my last sense of security. She would lie next to my bed at night and I felt safe. All of this loss in such a short time period was more than I could take. I felt totally abandoned and I emotionally caved in. I was not sure if I would be able to make it through these difficult times.

There were days when I felt that I was unable to pick my head up. How was I to be able to go to work to care for others as a nurse, when I could hardly stand up myself?

I sought strength in my daily prayer time. I asked God to help me endure the pain of the grief. My sorrow was compounded by the reality that I was rejected. This I found was an entirely different type of pain that I would have to deal with. To think that someone I loved chose to leave me. Not like my dad or my dog who were ill, but someone that I trusted and thought that they loved me, betrayed me and just left. That insult to my self worth caused excruciating pain that I did not know how to deal with.

What I needed reminded of was that I would not have to go through it alone. It was when I was reading the Word that the Lord helped me to realize that He was with me and that I was protected.

When I would feel vulnerable and lacking a sense of security, I found comfort in picturing my guardian angel standing at my left side. I named her Lily several years before and have an image in my mind of what she looks like. She stands at least eight feet tall, with large full-feathered wings and is very strong. I know that she is a mighty warrior and protects me in daily battles with the enemy. If necessary she can move very rapidly, and yet at other times she will patiently wait on me to catch up. Lily knows me very well, since she has been with me since my conception. She is someone that I can trust.

At my right side I imagine the Holy Spirit. Since my baptism the Holy Spirit has lived inside of me. This counselor advises me on a daily basis and is more than a conscience that tells me right from wrong. These two winged protectors take hold of me under my arms and gently lift me up, in spirit. I feel that my feet are about two inches above the ground. I won't trip on anything. It is as if my feet can glide just above ground level, making my daily walk easier for me. During those times when I need emotional support, my guardians will always stand beside me like my white knights in shining armor. They are strong, fearless, and unwavering.

In front of me walks Jesus. He is slightly bent over forward carrying my cross. He is watching and leading me through every step that I take. With the weight of my sins on His shoulder He walks ahead, looking back to make sure that I'm all right, and with a loving nod He shows me where to step. He is watching and leading me through every situation that I may face. He has taken the brunt of my load allowing me to walk freely. Jesus' eyes are watchful, aware of what is up ahead, but never pressuring; only gently guiding. With this reassurance, I realize that I have no need to fear the future. Jesus is walking ahead to prepare the way for me.

On my right shoulder, I feel the right hand of God. He is out of my sight, but His presence is known. "Not to worry My child," He seems to whisper in my ear, "I got your back." No one dares to stab me in the back while my Father is standing behind me. I am able to let go of the past, for what is done is done. Knowing that God is mighty, it is easy to picture that He is standing tall behind me with His head right above mine. He watches to my left and my right, and He holds me close to Him, as if to provide me with a second spine. Now with my shoulders back I am able to stand straight and hold my head up high, filled with the confidence that I am a child of God.

I refuse to believe the lie that I am totally alone. I once again feel loved and safe. You see I'm covered on all sides; what a relief! It gives me the courage that I need to carry on. And I am confident that you can feel the same. For the many times in your life that you have been hurt and when others disregard your feelings. When you have been rejected or betrayed. For the times that you feel that your best friend has just stabbed you in the back, or that you could have allowed someone to hurt you so badly. When you think of these things that had been done to you and how your heart ached, remember that we should not determine our worth based on how others treat us. But look for comfort in the fact that you have the Creator of the universe covering your back, the One who is Truth and is Love. Our sense of self worth should come from God.

> "No evil shall befall you, no affliction come near
> your tent.
> For God commands the angels to guard you in all
> your ways.
> With their hands, they shall support you,
> Lest you strike your foot against a stone."
> (Psalm 91:10-12) NKJV

> "The Lord is near to those who have a broken heart, and
> saves such as have a contrite spirit.
> (Psalm 34:18) NKJV

> "You hold my right hand. You guide me with your
> counsel"
> (Psalm 73:23-24) NKJV

THE CRUCIFIX

On the North Side of Pittsburgh is a small Catholic Chapel dedicated to Saint Anthony of Padua which houses over 5,000 relics. The Shrine has been designated a historical site by the Pittsburgh History and Landmarks Foundation. The resident nun who gives tours explains that one relic is a splinter of the cross that Christ was crucified on. There is also a thorn from the Crown of Thorns and a piece of stone from the Holy Sepulcher. All the relics have documentation to verify their authenticity which accompanied their acquisition.

Although the chapel is small, it has life size Stations of the Cross which line the outside walls. A large statue of St. Anthony is surrounded by hundreds of candles, the flickering of which gives an eerie glow to his silhouette. The reliquaries that house the relics are numbered for archiving and are made of pure gold. It is difficult to take it all in even when sitting and just slowly studying altar to altar.

Because of the chapel's size and the minimal lighting, the dimness allows a person to close their eyes and separate themselves from the outside world. You can almost feel the presence of the holy saints whose remains surround you.

I had visited this holy place only a few times but would make a point of stopping in its gift shop. There I had purchased two three-inch crucifixes that contained the Crucifix Medal of St. Benedict. I found myself carrying one of the crucifixes in my pocket at all times. Even though I had been to the Vatican and other churches in Rome, I feel that this chapel is one of the most sacred places that I have ever been to. I believe that is why I felt very blessed to carry a crucifix that I had associated with this sacred shrine.

During my separation from my husband, there were times when I was physically and emotionally drained. I found comfort praying while holding a crucifix in my hand. I started to place the crucifix in my pocket, and wherever I was, if I felt that I was going to emotionally break down and cry, I would squeeze my hand around it tightly and pray. It was always a reminder that God was with me. I don't know how it happened, but after several months of carrying my crucifix in my pocket, I lost it.

I checked every pair of slacks that I had, my coat pockets, purses, under furniture and in my car. I looked everywhere. I felt angry at myself for losing something that gave me such comfort. Another loss! I thought. For six days I searched, and finally I prayed to God one night before going to sleep to please bring back my crucifix.

The next day I went to work, and during lunch a secretary from another department joined us. Her husband had been diagnosed the year before with terminal cancer of the liver. I had given him the other crucifix six months before, and told him that I hoped that it would bring him comfort like mine had brought me. She went into her pocket and said to me. "Jim wanted me to give this back to you." As she handed me a small box she began to explain that he had appreciated my thoughtfulness, but he wanted me to have it back. It was coming to the end of his life, and he wanted to make sure that the crucifix was returned to me. So he sent it to me with his wife.

I could not believe it. I had asked God the night before to please bring my crucifix back. This crucifix was exactly the same as the one that I had lost. It never ceases to amaze me just how awesome our God is.

Sometimes you just need something to hold on to, and that for me was my crucifix. But I had become too attached and dependent on the crucifix itself and physically holding it in my hands. I lost sight of the true source of my strength. I believe it was for this reason that God permitted me to lose it. I came to realize that it was not the cross that was my comforter, but the sweet Savior who died on it for me.

> The LORD *is* the strength of my life;
> Of whom shall I be afraid?
> When the wicked came against me
> To eat up my flesh,
> My enemies and foes,
> They stumbled and fell..(Psalm 27: 1-2) NKJV

SOMETHING SPECIAL

My life was filled with a husband, two sons, two dogs, a full time job, a part-time job and demanding college courses. I actually thought I had squeezed in an adequate amount of time for God. But I was wrong. I guess that is why God needed to get my attention, and that He did!

After thirty years of marriage, I now found myself separated from my husband. I needed to ponder the reality of the recent trauma that had become my life. What had happened in my marriage made no sense to me. I had mentally dissected every aspect, but still did not understand. I physically felt a hole in my chest, directly over my heart.

The feeling of rejection seemed to eat away at my sense of worth. I began to question if I could ever be loved again. I started to read a number of self help books and began therapy with a personal counselor. But it wasn't until I made the effort to read scripture daily that I started to understand how much God loved me, and how He wanted to be involved in every aspect of my life. I was especially fond of the book of Job. I enjoyed reading how God responded to Job, reminding him of His greatness. I was encouraged when I read how God had planned for every aspect in everything that He created, something that I had never thought about. That assured me that He also had my entire life under His control. I also found the Psalms uplifting. When you give praise to God, it allows you to take your mind off your own problems. God, in turn, gives us a peace that only He can provide.

When I had experienced the loss of my husband, I found that my relationship with God had changed. I had seen in others how this type of loss had caused bitterness and a turning away from God. It was quite the contrary for me. I started to realize that if I was to get through this heart wrenching situation that was sadly now my life, I could not make it without the help of God.

During times when I needed to try to sort things out and there where many of them, I would go to a local park and walk the one mile track that outlined a man-made lake. I felt very safe there. I really enjoyed the fact that a portion of the path went through a canopy of deciduous trees. As soon as I entered this covered area, I was filled with calmness. The temperature dropped slightly offering a cool breeze, and outside sounds became buffered. These surroundings provided me with an escape from all the pain that I felt was devouring me ... I could feel peace and joy.

Many of the people that I passed in walking were wearing ear phones. It seemed a shame to me that they were depriving themselves of the sounds of nature that were all around them. I can see how this would allow walkers to isolate themselves from everyone they encountered along the way. Perhaps that was what they needed that day, but not me.

On one particular day, I made my usual trek around the path, making note of the family of ducklings splashing playfully. As they quacked loudly, I could only imagine what they were saying to each other. I was conscious of how good nature made me feel. It was an internal calming, a type of release for me. I took note of the vibrant color of the orange wild lilies, the different textures of the water, trees and sky. I looked everywhere for signs of God's thumb print.

I was feeling very happy as I turned the curve and spotted a bench that sat atop a hillside overlooking the lake. I decided to sit on the bench and take in the beautiful view. The sun was positioned at the opposite end of the lake. I found myself slightly squinting from the brightness, but the warmth felt great on my face. The sun had produced patches of glistening reflections randomly placed over the lake surface. I silently prayed to God, thanking Him for the privilege of this experience. I felt very blessed and close to Him and I felt the urge to ask Him for more. As I prayed, I made the request, "Show me something special, Lord." The words were barely out of my mouth when I saw the water's light reflections start to quickly move across its surface.

I watched the shape of the reflection as it formed a straight column perpendicular to me. Then the end that was closest to me started to expand outward. It all happened in a few seconds; the reflection had formed a giant arrow, approximately thirty-feet long and forty-feet wide at the pointed end. The best part of this was that the arrow was pointing directly at me! It was as if a giant neon light similar to those used to advertise was letting me know, "Here she is." What a gift! I could hardly believe my eyes. As quickly as it had happened, the reflection dispersed across the lake. I found myself grinning and then chuckling out loud.

We all look for signs from God, and I could never have imagined anything like this happening to me, but it did! It just goes to prove how great our God is. He is able to WOW us. I have promised myself that I will try to be more observant and thankful for the earthly gifts that the good Lord has given me.

I have decided to look at life differently. My eyes are starting to see things I never noticed before and my ears pick up on sounds that I used to ignore. And my heart is starting to understand. It's a process, and I know that I have a long way to go, but I am on my way.

There comes a time in everyone's life when we wonder what it would be like if we were just better looking, or thinner, or smarter. We may question if we are lovable. The problem is we are looking through the eyes of men. We need to look at ourselves through God's eyes. We need to remember that He sent His Son to die for us. He thinks we are all something special!

> "I have showed you this so that in Me you
> may have peace."
> (John 16:33) NKJV

THE TASSEL

Over the years I have tried several areas of my house to see where I feel the most comfortable praying. I looked for a place where there is the least amount of distractions and I am able to settle my mind from my everyday activity and focus on the Word. In the summer months I enjoy the chair on my back deck. I have a canopy of three trees that provide shade. The sound of bubbling water from my pond's waterfall is a soothing background sound for meditating. In the winter months, I have to settle for the comfort of a wing backed chair in my living room. The high sides of the chair seem to wrap around me, mimicking a hug. With feet up on an ottoman, I am able to read my bible and allow my heart and mind to receive God's words. A floor lamp sits next to the chair and on it hangs a four inch decorative tassel. I hung the tassel on the lamps extension arm that can stretch several inches out from the lamp's base.

On one occasion I was praying and decided to speak to my Guardian Angel Lily. I told Lily that I was wondering how powerful her wings were. I explained that I knew that she was a warrior and must be very strong. After all, our guardians are constantly in battle, fighting off the demons that try to rob us of our joy and peace. I started to joke with her and so I kiddingly dared her. I bet her that her wings were not powerful enough to move the tassel that hung from my lamp.

It was only a second later that the tassel slowly and gently moved back and forth. The tassel swayed from side to side for a full minute. I just started to laugh out loud. That's my Lily I thought. I was conscious of the fact that this movement did not frighten or upset me. Even though I had experienced an encounter with the spiritual world, I was not shaken; in fact, it felt quite natural to me.

A few months later I decided to ask Lily again to move the tassel. I was sitting in the chair and after reading the bible for a while, I began to speak to her. I told her that I felt that she was the best Guardian Angel that anyone could wish for. I told her that I really enjoyed seeing her move the tassel with her wings and I would love for her to move it again. Immediately the inside of the tassel started to move as if they were dancing. It was unbelievable! As I sat in the chair I could look up into the bottom of the tassel. The outside layer of the tassel strings were not moving just the inside ones and they were not moving back and forth they were moving up and down.

What a gift from my guardian when I asked her to show me that she was with me and she was permitted to respond. I found it very comforting in knowing that my angel has a sense of humor. Here is a spiritual being that has been with me since I was conceived. She knows me better than I know myself. Her power and might are something that I am unable to comprehend. And yet she playfully exhibited her presence to me. It is one thing to pray and acknowledge that you have an angel watching over you. It is totally awesome to share a moment of two way communication with them.

I was raised Roman Catholic, and have a distinctive memory of grade school nuns dressed in habits. They would smack wooden rulers on our desks, growling, as they warned that we should never mess with the spiritual world. Communicating with this unknown realm was just asking for trouble. I must admit that I agree with not wanting to invite evil demons into my life, but that never came to mind when I challenged Lily.

Our Angels are one of the many ways that God shows us that he cares for us. He has placed them by our sides to protect us throughout our walk on earth. When it is my time to leave this life, I am sure that Lily will be there to accompany me to heaven.

I encourage you to speak to your Guardian Angel. You never know what they are capable of until you acknowledge their presence.

"Are they not all ministering spirits,
Sent forth to minister for them who shall be heirs of
salvation?"
(Hebrews 1:14) NKJV

"See that you do not despise one of these little ones,
for I say to you that their angels in heaven always look
upon the face of my heavenly Father."
(Matthew:18:10)NKJV

"The angel of the LORD,
Who encamps with them,
Delivers all who fear God."
(Psalm34:7)NKJV

My Daily Word - Messages Of Hope

There was a time when I found it impossible to pray. I would read a sentence of scripture and not remember what I read once I got to the next line. I felt numb. It was almost like walking through a wall of Jell-O. All my senses were slower and less acute, and my ability to learn or retain information was at an all time low. At times when someone would speak to me, it would take a few minutes for the words to work their way from my ears to my brain where I could slowly process them.

I know that I had mentally formed an invisible "force field" around myself. It was my mind's way of protecting me from any more input. I was stunned and needed to slowly unravel the protective layers as if peeling the skin off an onion. I needed to feel loved and valued, secure from abandonment.

When I was unable to read scripture, I found myself on my knees, usually crying and begging God to help me. It was during these times that God acted in a unique manner. He spoke to me through a Daily Word book.

You may be familiar with the format of the book. There is usually a quote from scripture with a paragraph or two on a topic relating to the daily scripture. It was light reading, easy to understand, contrary to some scripture that I was battling to comprehend.

Now I know that it is considered foolish to open up the Bible and just point our finger to a verse and expect it to relate to our problem or meet our specific need. But in a way, that is just what the Lord did for me. I would pray for a while, and then ask Him to please speak to me regarding something special that was weighing heavily on my heart. Each time I prayed it was for something different. For example, I would ask for increased faith, or hope, understanding of relationships or finding forgiveness. And when I opened the Daily Word book, there it was, a full page of positive affirmations regarding God's involvement in that particular topic. This blessed type of communication continued for a year.

I know this sounds strange, but it is true. One day I had prayed over a topic, and when I opened the book and read the two pages neither applied to what I had asked about. For some reason, I laid the book down with the pages open. I went into the other room and when I returned and looked at the book, the pages were turned to two new pages which had scripture and two paragraphs discussing the topic that I was asking about. I know that this is difficult to believe, and if someone were to tell me that this happened to them, I must admit that I would be doubtful. But I'm telling you that all things are possible through God. You just need to trust Him and believe in Him.

Three years have passed and I am now able to find comfort in reading the Bible. So the need to refer to the inspirational book has not been as strong as it was. I have tried opening it and have not found the corresponding messages that I once did. I believe that there was a season when I truly needed to hear from God and that He met my need by reaching out to me in a very unique way. We all need God, and if we reach out to Him, He will find a way to let you know that He is there.

"Whatever things you ask in prayer,
Believing, you will receive"
(Matt: 21:22) NKJV

"If any of you lacks wisdom,
Let him ask of God,
Who gives to all liberally and without reproach,
And it will be given to him.
But let him ask in faith, with no doubting,
For he who doubts is like a wave of the sea driven and tossed by the wind."
(James 1:5-6) NKJV

www.ingramcontent.com/pod-product-compliance
Lightning Source LLC
Chambersburg PA
CBHW021920040426
42448CB00007B/831

* 9 7 8 1 4 2 6 9 3 3 4 6 2 *